W9-ATI-719

spot

CREEPY CRAWLIES

SPIDERS

by Nessa Black

AMICUS | AMICUS INK

eyes

web

Look for these words and pictures as you read.

legs

palps

Do you see that spider?
It is waiting.
It wants to catch food.

Look at the spider's eyes.
They see light and dark.
They see movement.

eyes

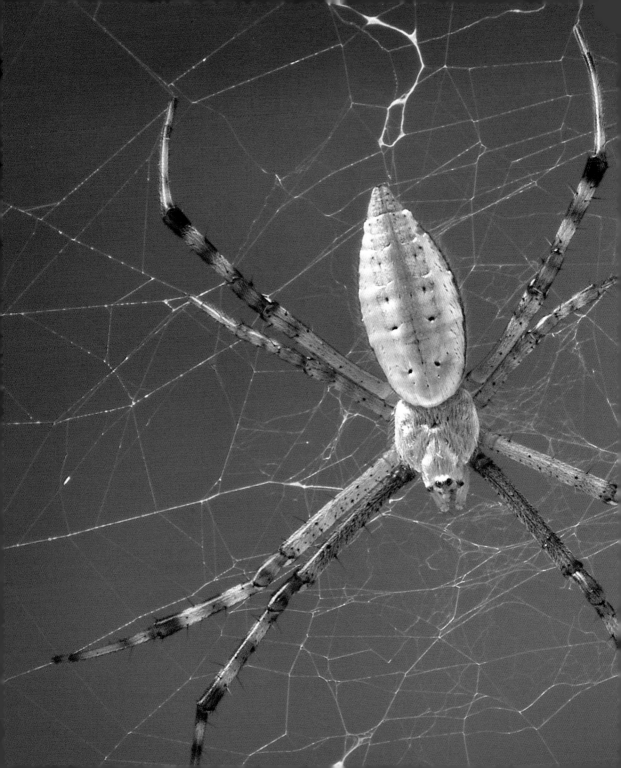

Look at the web.
It is sticky.
A bug gets stuck.

web

Look at the spider's legs.
They do not stick to the web.

legs

Look at the hairs on its legs.
Some hairs can smell.
Spiders can smell well.

Look at the spider's palps.
They are like little arms.
They push food into its mouth.
Yum!

palps

There are many kinds of spiders.
How many have you seen?

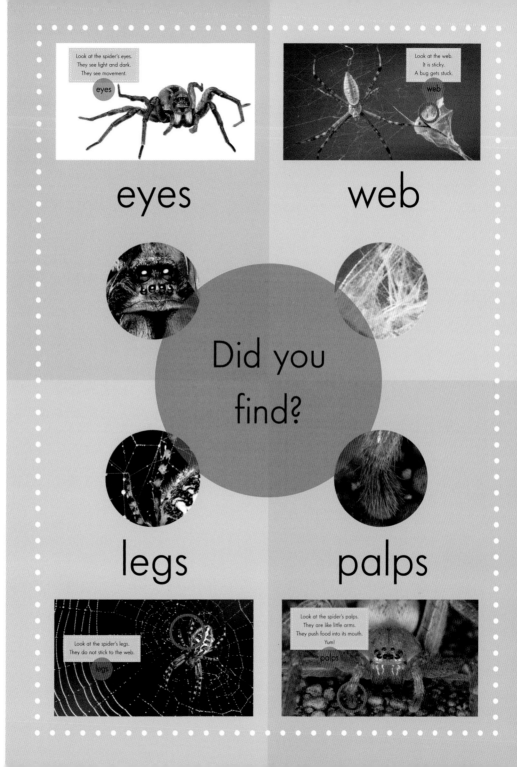

Look at the spider's eyes.
They see light and dark.
They see movement.

eyes

Look at the web.
It is sticky.
A bug gets stuck.

web

eyes

web

Did you find?

legs

palps

Look at the spider's legs.
They do not stick to the web.

legs

Look at the spider's palps.
They are like little arms.
They push food into its mouth.
Yum!

palps

spot

Spot is published by Amicus and Amicus Ink
P.O. Box 1329, Mankato, MN 56002
www.amicuspublishing.us

Library of Congress Cataloging-in-Publication Data
Names: Black, Nessa, author.
Title: Spiders / by Nessa Black.
Description: Mankato, Minnesota : Amicus, [2018] | Series:
   Spot. Creepy crawlies | Audience: K to grade 3.
Identifiers: LCCN 2016056176 (print) | LCCN 2016059954
   (ebook) | ISBN 9781681511108 (library binding) | ISBN
   9781681522296 (pbk.) | ISBN 9781681512006 (ebook)
Subjects: LCSH: Spiders--Juvenile literature.
Classification: LCC QL458.4 .B6345 2018 (print) | LCC
   QL458.4 (ebook) | DDC 595.4/4--dc23
LC record available at https://lccn.loc.gov/2016056176

Printed in China

HC 10 9 8 7 6 5 4 3 2 1
PB 10 9 8 7 6 5 4 3 2 1

Wendy Dieker, editor
Deb Miner, series designer
Ciara Beitlich, book designer
Holly Young, photo researcher

Photos by Age Fotostock 12–13;
iStock cover, 10–11; Shutterstock 1,
4–5, 6–7, 8–9, 14; SuperStock 3

SPIDERS